Mike,

Thank you for everything

you do for your

Students and

BULLYPROOF
Unleash the Hero Inside Your Kid

Your community to

be BULLYPROOF!

Alex

BULLYPROOF
Unleash the Hero Inside Your Kid
VOLUME 1

CONTRIBUTING AUTHORS:

TROY AUMAN

JUAN COLON

OSHEN DUNCAN

JO FULLER

SCOTT HERTZIG

RICHARD HILL

VEENU KELLER

ERIN LAURAINE

BRETT LECHTENBERG

JOHN NOTTINGHAM

EDITORS:

MICHAEL CUDDYER

ALEX CHANGHO

BULLYPROOF
Unleash the Hero Inside Your Kid

DEDICATION

To all the people out there who have ever been bullied: we have a chance to make a difference now.

To all the people out there who are currently being bullied: there is hope.

TABLE OF CONTENTS

FOREWORD

By Amit Bhargava, M.D.

Although the word "bully" can be traced back to the early 16th century, the practice of this socially unacceptable behavior most likely pre-dates this. In the mid 19th century, Darwin coined the phrase, "survival of the fittest," whilst describing his theory of evolution. Undoubtedly, the desire to survive is innate and common to all living things. However, this combined with a desire to compete or gain superiority over others results in actions that can be both physically and verbally abusive. Sadly, children, adolescents and even some adults, from all walks of life, may fall victim to this. Alarmingly, bullying is no longer a local or regional issue, but a global one. Mechanization and connectivity have given rise to entities like cyber bullying, which transcend physical boundaries and leave far deeper scars. Unfortunately, the visible effects of bullying, both physical and emotional, are only the tip of the iceberg. Those affected experience deep-rooted psychological distress that may manifest in years to come. Aside from the mental trauma and psychosocial imbalance that results from bullying, victims are at risk of developing a host of medical disorders. It is well established that bullying can lead to unhealthy behaviors like disordered eating.

Studies show us that individuals who have been bullied are at greater risk of developing obesity, diabetes and cardiovascular disease. These, in turn, decrease quality of life, increase morbidity and may even be life threatening.

Having said this, it is high time to put an end to bullying. We as individuals, as parents, and as members of the society, must come together and protect not only ourselves, but our greatest assets...our children. *BULLYPROOF: Unleash the Hero Inside Your*

Kid is the first step in the right direction. Put together by experts in community, this series gives parents practical and usable advice, that not only helps them understand the ramifications of bullying, but teaches them how to empower their children to stand up to its effects and come out stronger than before. Instilling this inner strength in our children is crucial to ensuring their mental, psychosocial and metabolic well-being. It is only by standing together, and being part of the solution, that we can hope to make the world a safer and better place for us and our subsequent generations. With this in mind, I implore you to pick up a copy, read the lessons contained within, and Unleash the Hero Inside Your Kid!

Dr. Amit Bhargava completed his fellowship in Endocrinology, Diabetes and Metabolism at the University of Connecticut, and is certified by the American Board of Internal Medicine. Whilst being trained in the entire gamut of Endocrinology, his special interests include the management of diabetes mellitus, obesity, bone and mineral disorders, osteoporosis, pituitary disorders and thyroid dysfunction. He has done extensive research and written several papers in the field of Endocrinology, which have been published in international journals in both Europe and the United States of America.

Dr. Bhargava currently serves as Senior Consultant at the Fortis Memorial Institute and Research Center in India.

MB BCh BAO (NUI, RCSI), LRCP & SI (Hons., Royal College of Surgeons in Ireland)

MD (Baystate Medical Center/TUFTS University School of Medicine)

Fellow in Endocrinology, Diabetes and Metabolism (University of Connecticut)

ABIM Board Certified in Internal Medicine and Endocrinology, Diabetes and Metabolism

INTRODUCTION: WHY LUKE SKYWALKER ISN'T MY HERO (ANYMORE)

BY ALEX CHANGHO
APEX, NORTH CAROLINA

When I was 5 years old, I was obsessed with Star Wars.

I *loved* Luke Skywalker. He was my hero. He has a lightsaber, and he flew through the galaxy fighting the bad guys. He was brave, he was bold. He did good. And he seemed fearless. I wanted to be

Luke Skywalker. He was my hero. This might sound typical for a young boy. But for me, it was a little different. See, it was different because... when I was young, *I didn't want to be me.*

I'm Alex Changho. And, if you've met me, you know I'm Asian. And not because of the obvious... yes, of *course* I look that way. But you could be blind and still know. I talk about being Asian, I make jokes about it, I use self-deprecating humor.

And while for some people, this kind of behavior might be a sign of low self-esteem, I'm pretty proud of my heritage.

But it wasn't always this way.

I grew up in Leawood, Kansas, a suburb of Kansas City. Smack-dab in the heart of the American Midwest, it wasn't the most ethnically diverse metropolis around (it still isn't). At my school, there were four Asian kids (me, my sister, and my two cousins), two black kids (Sara and Joseph, who were adopted with white parents), and everyone else was white.

Not to say that I was bullied because of my race when I was little. In fact, I wasn't. But... I knew. I knew I was different. My hair was different, my eyes were slanted, and I didn't have a name like "Smith" or "Williams." My grandmother, who lived with us, didn't speak English. So, of course, I spoke Chinese.

Now, today in 2015 that might seem like a really cool thing for a 5 year old kid. For me growing up, it was just another reminder of how different I was.

That sensitivity to being different led me to be less confident, regardless of my school grades, how many friends I had, or anything else. Because I wanted to be like everyone else. I didn't want to be different. I didn't want to be me.

It's this lack of personal confidence that led to the challenges I had, and when bullying became a problem for me. My bullies showed up in the fourth grade.

There's a distinction though: bullying was never the problem. It was the *effect* that bullying was having on me that left me feeling bad, feeling self-conscious, and wishing I was the same as everyone else.

Bullying has been around since the days of Cain and Abel. Bullying is almost a natural feature of society, something that, while not great, is part of being human. Bullying is a behavior that people will do because it meets several needs.

Tony Robbins teaches that there are six human needs: the need for certainty and control; the need for variety and newness; the need for love and connection; the need for significance; the need to grow; and the need to contribute.

He also establishes that every single human being will engage in behaviors to need said needs, and that if a behavior meets three or more, then it becomes an addiction.

What needs could bullying meet for a person?

- The need for certainty and control – a bully can control a situation, or try to control the people around him
- The need for variety – bullying behavior can have multiple targets with multiple responses from people
- The need for connection – getting in somebody's face can connect you with them; as well as connecting with others when a group bullies a person
- The need for significance – bullying someone makes the bully very significant in the eyes and mind of the target

It's clear that bullying behaviors will persist as long as humans have needs.

So the problem, then, is not bullying in itself, but the *effects* that bullying has on people. If a bully chooses a target, but that target does not respond in a way that meets the bully's needs... then the bullying will eventually stop. This, and the target is unaffected.

It's not about stopping bullying – it's about making people bullyproof.

The bullying will continue, but we, together, can help empower more boys and girls, more teenagers, and more men and women to have a higher level of self-esteem, self-worth, and personal confidence.

It's when a person *lacks* this, then bullying will be a problem.

Back to the fourth grade...

Shy, skinny Alex Changho moves to North Carolina and attends public school. He knows no one there, and is still one of just a handful of Asian kids. But there are black kids, white kids, Hispanic kids. And I just don't seem to fit in.

I wasn't hip with the black kids, I didn't speak Spanish and I definitely wasn't white. My own personal esteem was at such a level that, even if other kids didn't racially profile, I was sensitive to it anyway.

And the consequences...

- I was picked on in the 4th grade, because I was nerdy

- I was picked on in the 5th grade, because I was Asian

- I was bullied in the 6th and 7th grades, partially because I was in the 6th grade, but particularly because of my race.

Now, I had been taught like a good little boy to do the usual things. "Ignore them." "Tell the teacher." "Sticks and stones can break your bones, but words can never hurt you."

Well you know what... when you've got low self-esteem, and you're in the 7th grade, and you have no friends... all of that is *bullshit.*

Words will pierce someone's heart and hurt you in a way that a busted lip, a broken arm, or a black eye will *never* compare to.

Because it's all encompassing. It affects a person's identity. It stays with you. Physical pain will go away as the body heals. Healing the heart is a completely different story.

This is why it is so vital that a person, whether kid or adult, is given the opportunity to become empowered, and have a level of confidence and esteem that is high enough to withstand the inevitable onslaught of teasing, picking on, and bullying.

If you lived in South Florida, which is subject to several hurricanes each year, would you choose to live in a flimsy shack on the beach? And if you did, could you blame nature for your shack blowing over every time a storm comes through? Of course not, you would build a stronger, more study home. One that is hurricane-proof.

Well let's do the same thing with your kid. Make them bullyproof.

When I was in the 5th grade, my parents put me in martial arts. Like a lot of the authors in this first volume, martial arts changed my life and helped me *feel confident.*

I'm not going to tell you how martial arts did it for me, or try to persuade you to do martial arts. But here's what I know: *because I felt my inner confidence, my life changed.*

I walked differently.

People came to me to talk, instead of me having to go to them.

I felt more comfortable in groups of people I didn't know.

I was attractive to women.

I was less afraid to try things, to pursue my goals, and to work for the things I believed in.

It wasn't an overnight thing. It took *years*. Years of practice, doing things over and over again, facing challenges, overcoming them, getting hurt, falling down, getting up again, breaking through obstacles.

There was no quick fix, no "come to my bully-prevention seminar and your life will change forever." I worked on myself weekly for years.

And after all that, I was more confident, more proud of who I was as a person.

I was proud to be me.

This is what being bullyproof is all about.

I'm blessed to be joined by contributing authors who are experts in working with kids. Many, like me, have dedicated their lives to teaching martial arts and changing lives in the way mine was. Others, from different industries, bring their own unique and powerful perspectives. We have a medical doctor, who I've known since the 8th grade, who I know was picked on as a kid; we have an expert in working with children and families, using NLP and personal development; we have the leading expert in personal safety in Utah; we have an expert in personal protection and defense; and of course, we have a number of martial arts professionals who are on the front lines, helping kids become bullyproof.

They share their experiences so you can work with your own family to empower them.

Like me, a lot of kids love super heroes. It's great to see kids want to be like someone else, like a hero. It's even better when they see that hero inside themselves.

At the time this book is being published, Star Wars Episode VII is about to be released. And when it comes out, I'm going to see it. Not because Luke is my hero... but because he's a hero just like me.

Alex Changho is a lifestyle and business coach. With almost two decades of experience leading and motivating others, and running a business, he helps business owners integrate their life's mission and career with their personal side of their life.

An accomplished speaker and presenter, Alex is a Master NLP Practitioner and Trainer, Senior Leader with Anthony Robbins, and Master Strengths Coach.

Alex lives in North Carolina with his wife, Kathleen, and his cat Bert.

For more information, visit www.alexchangho.com.

CHAPTER 1: EXPERIENCING LIFE WITH BULLYING

BY VEENU KELLER
JACKSONVILLE, NORTH CAROLINA

I think that my contribution to this book may be a little bit different than others you'll read. My profession is what some people call a life coach, but I prefer to call myself more of a behavioral coach. In my work I specialize in a number of very focused groups. One of my main focuses is on bullying, and specifically suicide prevention in people who experience bullying. I work with kids who have experienced bullying and help them recover things they've lost in the process, like self-esteem and a feeling of self-worth.

It's scary the number of bullying victims I see each year, and I'm happy to be able to help as many as I can. Bullying, as well as suicide prevention related to bullying, is a topic that's quite close to my heart. In addition to the academic, psychology, and behavioral training that I've used to develop an expert level of knowledge about bullying and bully prevention, I also have personal experiences with bullying that give me a unique and important perspective on things like mental illness, depression, suicide, and other terrible effects that bullying can cause.

Before getting into my own experiences, I'd like to share my thoughts on what a bully is. This is an important aspect of bullying, I think, because it's one that's often overlooked. For example, when bullying occurs in a school the first instinct is to focus on the victim. This is how it should be, but once the victim is identified and begins the process of getting help we sort of drop the ball on where the issue originates - the person doing the bullying. When parents call me for help, it's usually the parents of the bullying victim. It's never the parents of the bully calling up to say, "Hey, my kid's a bully, can you help them?" This is a bit alarming because the bully is the source of the problem, yet little emphasis is placed on that piece of the puzzle.

So what is a bully? In my experience a bully is someone who lacks self-esteem and self-worth, and seeks to take those things from someone else in order to compensate for their shortcomings. Think about this - if you have self-esteem, if you have self-worth, if you know who you are, then why would you try to take those things away from someone else? That's what bullying is, that's what bullies do - they take what they need from their victims. They rob others of their self-worth to add to their own to feel like they're better than they are. Understanding this dynamic and paying attention to how bullies operate allows us to take the time to talk to both bullies and victims, and have them ask themselves the questions of "Why do I bully?" and "Why do I allow myself to be bullied?" respectively.

Bullying Finds Me

I mentioned that I have a personal connection with bullying. I think it's important for me to share my story with you as a way to gain a deeper understanding of what bullying can do to a person, and the lingering effects it can have.

My parents came from India to the US, where I grew up in southern California with my brother as the first generation in my family to be born here. My parents actually divorced when I was very young, which is very unusual for an Indian family, and my mother raised my brother and me herself. Living in California you may think that I was in the melting pot of the world where everyone is diverse and used to different cultures, but the school I attended was predominantly white with only a handful of Hispanic and African American children. My brother and I were the only Indians in the school, actually, and that's where I had my first experience with bullying.

Some kids have their first taste of bullying as they get a bit older, but I had mine when I was six years old. I remember being treated differently by the teacher, and beginning to think that I was different very early on. I started feeling like there was something wrong with me, and soon kids started calling me the "N" word. I was confused because I wasn't black, but in their minds it was a hurtful thing they could say to someone with darker skin than their own. They also started calling me "dot head", and one boy even poked me in the middle of the forehead while he said that to me. That's when it started sinking in - people didn't like me because of my skin color, something I had no control over. It was a helpless and hopeless feeling.

It got worse as things progressed to one of the most traumatic experiences of my youth. I had a few friends, and we'd play a game at recess where the boys would chase the girls and the girls would chase the boys. One day I caught one of the boys, and as I grabbed his arm he turned to me and said the ugliest, most hateful things. Really, things you can't even imagine a child saying. I won't repeat them here because of how explicit they were, but I'll never forget how I felt hearing those words directed towards me. I forced a smile and refused to cry in front of people, but I certainly cried later at home when they couldn't see me.

Even at home, though, I wasn't safe from bullying. When I told my mother what happened she just said, "Kids will be kids", and not to worry about it. I already felt alone, and now my own mother seemed to be siding with the people who'd hurt her daughter. My grandmother offered even less comfort, making me feel as different at home as I felt at school. As an example, my skin has always been dark. When I was eight or nine my grandmother put me in a bath and told me she needed to "scrub the color off" of me. So at eight or nine years old I felt outcast and rejected by my social peers *and* my family, and that's when I can look back and say my depression really began.

Growing Up

As I got older, things continued to get worse. I remember walking home from school with kids following me to throw rocks while calling me obscene names. I felt like less than nothing, over and over again, day in and day out. My mom was a single mother, so I'd get home and be alone, crying by myself in isolation. I lived in constant fear of bullying, and fear that no one would ever like me let alone love me. I only had one "boyfriend" all the way through high school, and he broke up with me after only a few dates because he was being bullied in the locker room just for dating me. To protect himself he made up a reason for breaking up with me, which made me feel even worse.

That's the point that I became suicidal, because I didn't feel like life was worth living. There was nobody in my life, nobody that loved me. That's really what it comes down to - bullying strips us of our self-worth, making us feel like the world would be no different with us or without us because no one cares if we live or die. We all want significance, to feel wanted, to feel that we're worth something. Starting at the age of six I never felt that. I knew my mom loved me, I had a few friends, but none of it was enough to fill the void left by everything bullying stole from me. So I decided to kill myself. I was just about to swallow a bottle of prescription pills my mom had in our home when a friend showed up and stopped me. To this day I don't know how he got there when he did, or where he is today, but I'll never forget him.

After that I was checked into a mental hospital for two months for being "emotionally detached", or whatever term they used for it back then. While I was in the hospital I learned cutting from watching other people's behavior, and I once I tried it I thought it was great. I'd cut, and the outside pain would take away the pain I felt inside. Even better, I could hide it from other people and they had no idea what was going on. I felt better, and kept it up for about a year in order to cope with everything.

Adults Aren't Immune

I'd like to be able to say that once I finished High School everything magically became wonderful for me, but that wouldn't be sharing my full story. What actually happened was when I was eighteen I met a Marine who said he loved me, and we married five months after we met. I believe that the years of bullying I went through took away all self-worth and certainty in my life, and with no loving connections I instantly married this man just because finally somebody loved me. Finally someone thought I had self-worth, but it didn't matter because I still didn't see it in myself. He would tell me I was beautiful, but I couldn't accept it because even if he believed it I never did. I hated the way I looked, I hated who I was, and the bullying I experienced in my life continued to gnaw at me even as an adult, keeping those suicidal thoughts in my mind.

I had a plan, though. At thirty-four years old I had two beautiful boys and I had divorced my husband. My plan was that I would wait until my boys were eighteen, and then I was done. My family wouldn't need me anymore, I wouldn't be leaving them with their father, and I'd finally be able to finish what I'd started so many years earlier. Ironically, throughout it all, I was working as a mental health professional. That is how great people are at hiding this stuff. Nobody knew my past, nobody knew I was bullied, nobody knew I was suicidal, and yet I was helping other people work through their emotional and mental health needs.

How I'm Still Here

So there I was at thirty-four, a lifetime of mental anguish ready to boil over, and someone invited me to a three day seminar. I wasn't going to go, I really didn't see the point, but that seminar was life altering. I'm not suggesting that it's what everyone needs, but I went through a process of self-discovery during that seminar that changed my life. When I got home after the seminar the first thing I did was walk upstairs to my room, look in the mirror, and say, "I love you". It was the hardest and most rewarding thing I have ever done in my life.

In that moment I finally realized what I'd needed for all those years. I fell in love with myself, and it was a feeling I never felt before. I didn't know that kind of love before then, and it was amazing. And what's interesting is that after you love yourself, you start to see all the people around you that really love you, and for the first time you can believe it and can enjoy it. I finally stopped letting myself be a victim, stopped letting people take things from me that were mine and that I deserved to keep. I was finally able to understand what my identity was, and start living my life on my terms.

Becoming Bullyproof

Now that I've shared my personal experiences, I'd like to share some ideas I have about how to combat bullying. Hopefully this will help others so they don't have to go through the same things as I did. First, the best piece of advice I can give both from my own experience with bullying as well as the kids I've worked with over the years is it all starts at home. For me, things might have been a lot different if my mom handled things another way. Like I said, I know she loved me and she did the best she could as a single mom in a foreign country who was raising two kids while earning a law degree, but she wasn't present with me. There were so many signs I gave about my issues that nobody saw.

So be present with your child, and pay attention to what is happening in their lives. If your present and involved in their lives you'll see your child crying, you'll see if your child is becoming withdrawn. You'll know better than to accept their claim that "Oh, no, I'm ok". By being present and knowing them, you'll know immediately if they're really ok or not. Make an effort to find out what's happening in their lives, I promise it will be worth it every time.

Another thing to do at home is tell your kids, everyday, that you're grateful for them. What does that do? It sets in their minds that someone loves them, that someone appreciates their presence in the world and is glad they're in it. Imagine all these kids that are being bullied, imagine if they all felt that someone was grateful for them. How different would their life be with that one little change? How different, by realizing that they're more than what other people might want them to think? Remember, a bully is someone who tries to take away things like self-esteem and self-worth. If they're going to try to take it, we need to teach kids to be strong enough to never give those things up, and we can do that by building those good feelings up as much as we can. And don't forget that the need for self-worth isn't isolated to children. It's something teens and adults have to have, as well. Once you know how much you're worth, nobody can ever take that away from you - nobody can make you less. So start by building these feelings up in children and letting it grow and develop throughout their lives.

Advice to Victims of Bullying

If you yourself are having bullying issues, it's never too late to decide who you are, take your identity back, and take the steps you need to take to realize you're worth something. Ask yourself these questions: What would have to happen for you to feel like a great person? What would have to happen for you to feel beautiful? What would have to happen for you to know that you're liked and loved? Answer these questions for yourself, not for others, and go after your own self-worth. It all starts with you. Whatever it takes, find something to fall in love with about yourself - maybe it's your heart, your sense of humor, the way you care about people, your eye color - just find something to fall in love with about yourself and let it blow up and become even bigger. Once you start letting yourself feel that way it will be a whole new start for yourself.

Advice to Parents of Bullying Victims

For parents who are watching their kids being bullied, it's hard. I know it's hard. I think that if I had to watch my child being bullied it would be harder for me than what I experienced going through bullying myself. The number one thing I'd do is let my child know I love them, and that we'll get through it together. I'd also take the time to figure out why the bullying is happening. I'd ask questions like: What is the bully saying to you? When are they saying it to you? I'd ask if my child knew anything about the bully's life, background, home life, etc. The truth is we never really know the whole story, but the bully is probably acting this way out of a coping mechanism and the more information we have the better prepared we can be to resolve the issues.

I hope my personal story about bullying helps people to understand how important an issue it is in our world, and how terrible and lasting the effects can be. Now that I've moved on it's all just like a story to me now, something from my past that doesn't define me but that I learned from. It's a story that I lived and I understand, so when I work with children who are dealing with bullying I can tell them I lived that life, I walked in their shoes. I know what it feels like to be alone, but I also know how it feels to break free of that despair and recreate an identity of strength. I truly believe that we can cure this poison that is bullying. By focusing on self-worth, both for ourselves and for our children, we can in fact create a world that is bullyproof.

Resources

In case you're interested in some resources, there are a few I'd recommend. The seminar that was my key moment was called *Unleash the Power Within* by Tony Robbins. That seminar also has a special youth group so teens can attend. They also have a youth camp called *Global Youth Leadership Summit* where teens from fourteen to eighteen can get some great leadership skills that really help with identifying themselves. I also conduct seminars, and I'd be happy to speak if anyone has a group or event that they'd like me to attend.

For over 5 years, Veenu Keller has worked with teens and adults to inspire them to believe in themselves and to know they always have a choice. Veenu has spent the last two decades working with at-risk teens, children with disabilities and parents of children with behavioral issues, drawing on her own experiences to coach people to aspire to want more and be more.

Veenu graduated with honors with a Bachelors in Psychology, and she was worked with a Teens in Transition program for five years. She has also completed a certification in coaching through Robbins-Madanes Training and is in the Senior Leadership Program with Tony Robbins.

When growing up, Veenu struggled to believe in herself and made choices that carried serious consequences, including inflicting self-harm through cutting and making a plan to commit suicide.

Today, Veenu shares her story with others to help them make better choices and become their own #1 fans. Veenu's story will have you crying, laughing and living her journey, but most of all she will have you believing in yourself.

For more information, visit www.veenuinspires.com.

CHAPTER 2: DEFINING BULLYING

BY TROY AUMAN & SCOTT HERTZIG
MANHATTAN, KANSAS

In the last few years bullying has been an increasingly hot topic with some really tragic events happening. We've worked to establish ourselves as local experts in order to do our part to prevent even more tragedies from happening, and also to work on bully prevention in general. At our martial arts school we specialize in teaching both children and adults the character traits and self-defense skills necessary to combat bullying. Although the increased discussion about bullying in the media has heightened awareness, it's important that people continue to educate themselves on what bullying is and how they can prevent it on a more personal scale at their local level. National coverage may not show all of the important details about bullying that a parent should know, so a great way to bullyproof a child is to be as informed as possible.

What is Bullying?

Along with bullying getting so much press coverage lately there have also been naysayers who don't seem to acknowledge bullying as much of a problem. This might be because the label of "bullying" gets put on many different behaviors, not all of which actually should be considered actual bullying. To us, bullying is a continuous, unwanted behavior that is done for the purposes of hurting someone else emotionally or physically. Bullying is also repetitive, something a person does over and over again.

You see, if somebody makes fun of another person a single time it's really not a bullying situation. We'd consider that more teasing, actually. Bullying and teasing are often confused, but the reality is that most kids actually tease each other pretty equally. Teasing is more a one-off type of behavior, or kids saying things back and forth without really meaning any harm. Now there is a fine line there where teasing can become bullying, and that goes for adults, too. We always explain to our students that it's also not just a matter of what you say, but how you say it. However, there's definitely a difference between showing bully-type behavior towards someone and just being rude.

Intention and Repetition

Another way to define if a behavior constitutes as bullying is to look at the intention and motive behind the behavior. Bullying is deliberate - it's a repeated pattern of behavior over time that is intended to cause harm. Bullying isn't arguing about who had what first, or saying a seat is taken because it's saved for another student, or accidentally bumping into someone and knocking them or their things over. With so much information out there about bullying lately, we see that kids are experiencing some common misconceptions about things like this where they think what they're witnessing or experiencing is bullying.

Again, though, bullying isn't one-off or accidental behavior - it's intentional and repeated. Arguing about who had something first isn't bullying, but being slapped in the face because of the argument might be. Saying a seat is being saved isn't bullying, but making it impossible for a student to sit and eat their lunch might be. Accidentally bumping into someone isn't bullying, but shoving a kid into a locker definitely is. These are all deliberate actions that warrant a bullying label. The difference in these examples is that the bullying behaviors are done with malicious intent, with the goal of embarrassing or hurting another person.

We also mentioned that bullying is repetition. Another way of saying this is that bullying shows a pattern of behavior that we can actually follow. Sometimes this pattern is easy where a bully picks on the same kid every day, pushing him around, making fun of him - that's an easy pattern to follow. It's clear that the bully is repeating a pattern with an intention of causing physical or emotional harm. Where it becomes a little murkier is when the bully changes targets and alters the pattern. Maybe our bully picks on Johnny on Monday, Billy on Tuesday, Jack on Wednesday, and so on. It's still a repeated pattern of bullying because although the targets are changing the behavior is repeated. This is actually something we often see with bullies, that it's very common for them to choose multiple targets.

This seemingly random selection of targets also makes it difficult to understand why bullies do what they do. We've talked about the motive behind bullying, the intention of doing harm to another person, but beyond that bullies don't really seem to need a reason for what they do. The intention is to harm, but the reason why they have that intention can be hard to define. It could be that the bully has been bullied themselves, at home or elsewhere, and they're looking for a way to compensate. It could also be one of hundreds of other possible reasons and there's really no way to know without further study of each individual bully. What we can say for certain is that the main factors in determining if a situation is bullying are the intention behind the behavior along with the frequency and repetition of said behavior.

So How Big a Problem is Bullying?

True bullying is a major problem in our world and it's happening all the time. Statistics show that one in three kids are bullied, with most occurrences happening in schools. It makes sense - kids spend a huge portion of their lives in schools and teachers can't be next to every kid every minute of every day. Take a moment to think about how scary that is, though. In a family with four children, statistically speaking, at least one of those kids will be a target at some point.

Knowing those statistics, now consider the side effects of bullying. Some of these side effects include depression, low self-esteem, health problems, poor grades, and in extreme circumstances suicide. In our martial arts school we've seen firsthand the ways bullying can have a monumental impact on a person, and the way being bullied can fundamentally change a person. The physical wounds of bullying usually don't take long to heal, but the mental and emotional effects can last a lifetime. This information is quite scary, and illustrates the fact that bullying truly is a huge problem.

The Evolution of Bullying

We all hear about times being different and how everything changes. Bullying isn't immune to the passage of time and has evolved quite a bit in recent years. The majority of bullying incidents are still being reported in schools, but with the digital age exploding around us the prevalence of social media has added to the bullying discussion. While face-to-face bullying will probably never go away, the advent of social media has created a new form of bullying called cyber-bullying where a bully can attack from the safety and isolation of their computer.

Another example of how bullying has evolved is the rise in incidents of bullying through social exclusion. This form of bullying is basically a group of kids making another kid feel unwanted or unaccepted in the group. It's not that it's a new form of bullying - it's actually been around for many years. What we're seeing, though, is that it's becoming more common in this technologically advancing era. With so many social apps available for kids to use it's become easier than ever to create cliques and purposefully make people feel excluded.

What Can You Do?

Now that we've taken some time to dissect bullying and get a better understanding of it we can talk about some strategies to help make kids bullyproof. First of all, let's go over what doesn't work. There are some ideas that parents have told us they've tried that are - well, let's just say they didn't work. Sending anonymous letters or messages to bullies, especially older ones, is not a good solution. Not only does it not work, but also by communicating directly with a kid you're actually putting yourself in a potentially hazardous legal situation. Also, forcing one kid to apologize to another is completely meaningless if the deeper issues haven't been resolved. Another idea that we've been seeing a lot of lately is this thing called "Verbal Karate", which is basically confronting a bully with words. Honestly, this kind of confrontation in an already heated situation is just adding fuel to the fire, and is also completely meaningless in the long run. Finally, some parents think they should just let their kid handle bullying on their own because "it builds character". That kind of thinking infuriates us because it's very narrow-minded, and quite scary that some people are actually teaching that to their kids.

Kids shouldn't be left to handle dangerous situations on their own - they should be encouraged to seek help and advice from their parents and teachers. In turn, the best thing parents can do for long-term results is to empower a kid who is being bullied with the right skills so they know how to react if they're bullied. Kids should also be taught strong values like self-esteem, confidence, pride, and a sense of self-worth. In our experience we've seen that kids who have these values taught on a regular basis are the least likely to be targeted by bullies in the first place. We suggest partnering your efforts with an activity or group that focuses on building these life-skills regularly, and in our opinion martial arts schools are terrific places to start.

Another thing parents can do to help bullyproof their kids is to know what their schools are doing to combat bullying. One of us, (Troy), is also a schoolteacher. As a result, we're able to get an inside look at how bullying is being handled, and the increased awareness and focus of anti-bullying initiatives. Teachers these days are going through a lot more training to get a better understanding of the different types of bullying, where it happens, how it happens, and what is and isn't actual bullying. Many programs being adopted by schools take the training to another level, incorporating support staff, janitors, and even parents in the training to make everyone more prepared to handle bully-type behaviors and situations. No one can fix the problem of bullying overnight, but with a combined effort between schools and families we can strive to continually get better.

We always say that you can lock your car overnight, but there's no guarantee that somebody won't try to get in. The point we're trying to make here is that there is no absolute solution to eliminating bullying, but we can take steps to do everything we can to try and make a difference. One of the best steps a parent can take to bullyproof their child is to be as informed as possible. That means taking the time to learn about bullying - what it is, how it works - as well as what your local schools are doing and how their policies affect your child. Finally, providing your child with tools that can keep them from being seen as a victim is a great way to bullyproof them, and we encourage you to seek out people and activities that will help with that goal.

Troy Auman is a 6th degree black belt, Internationally Certified Master Instructor with the American Taekwondo Association and Certified Instructor with Krav Maga Alliance. He has been training in martial arts since 1990 and has been running the Manhattan ATA since 1997.

He has also been a licensed school teacher with Manhattan Catholic Schools since 1999.

For more information, visit www.atakansas.com.

Scott Hertzig is a 4th degree black belt and an Internationally Certified Instructor with the American Taekwondo Association. He has been training since 1992 and has been teaching at Manhattan ATA since 2007.

For more information, visit www.atakansas.com.

CHAPTER 3: DEALING WITH BULLYING AT HOME

BY JUAN COLON
WINTER SPRINGS, FLORIDA

I've spent a great deal of my life developing skills that make me an

expert in martial arts. In addition to being an expert in martial

arts I also consider myself to be an expert in working with

children, especially when it comes to the subject of bullying.

Bullying is one of the most important issues facing children today,

and more than ever parents must maintain high levels of

awareness about bullying and bully prevention to protect their children.

I imagine that everyone has a slightly different idea of what bullying is. For me, bullying is the outward action someone takes when they have low self-esteem. It's human nature for someone to want to feel some measure of control in their lives, especially if they're in a situation where they feel hopeless or powerless. So many times what I see happening is this person who feels powerless then has a need to exert control somewhere. The bully can't control a situation in their own life so they seek someone weaker to compensate for their lack of self-esteem and self-confidence. This may manifest itself in being generally mean, trying to pick fights with someone who seems weaker, or just continually going at someone. The behavior continues because bullies tend to focus their energy on the targets who don't fight back.

Another factor that drives bullying is the way in which society treats it. There are still those with the attitude that an incident of bullying can simply be chalked up to "boys being boys". Too often we see proof that bullying has been taken for granted, as evidenced by the number of suicides that have been directly linked to it. What people need to understand is that bullying is everywhere - in the workplace, at school, on the Internet - and many times it happens behind closed doors. In fact, one common form of bullying that tends to be grossly underestimated is bullying in the home.

Bullying in the Home

When I discuss about bullying it's not just the stories and experiences of the children and families that I've worked with that I can cite, my own experiences as well. I've always had a smaller build, and as a child that made me a target. The first memory I have of being bullied happened when I was four years old. My bully wasn't on the schoolyard, and cyber bullying wasn't around yet. Instead, my very first bully was my cousin, a close family member.

The way it happened was that my aunt and cousin were visiting my family's house for the summer. My cousin was two years younger than me, but he was big for his age and was actually big enough to hurt me because I was so small. My aunt would wait for the rest of the family to leave and once we were alone she'd have my cousin fight me. She thought it was funny to see how weak I was, and I remember her laughing as I was getting hit. I was never an aggressive person, even as a child, and I just took the beating. As a result, I spent a lot of my childhood with lingering fear, self-doubt, and dangerously low levels of confidence and self-esteem.

While my own story may not be the same for everyone, the bigger point is that the bullying I faced happened in what should have been a safe environment. It was bullying by a family member, and it happens a lot more often than people think. The person doing the bullying could be an adult or a cousin, but some of the most common home bullying situations can be seen with siblings.

Siblings are in a unique situation in that they're essentially always around one another. They live together, participate in activities together, spend time together alone and in groups, etc. Because of all of this it has to be expected that siblings will argue, yell, and fight as they grow up. When we consider the idea of siblings bullying other siblings it has to be understood that there is a difference between what can be viewed as typical sibling rivalry and actual bullying. Bullying is what happens when things escalate to the point where one sibling is in a situation of feeling afraid, threatened, unsafe, or has real and lasting effects on their self-esteem and confidence as a result of the bullying. When things get to this point it's important to recognize and rectify the behaviors.

Another consideration about bullying in the home is that it can come from adults, even parents. In fact, one of the most common things I've seen actually is that bullying starts from the parents and how they act towards their children. Oddly enough, parents don't always see the ways their behavior could be considered bullying until they take a step back and really look at it from the outside. I don't mean to imply that all parents are bullies by any means, but consider what it means to be a bully based on my earlier definitions.

Think about this - a father has a bad day at work because his boss yelled at him and he had nowhere to vent. He comes home in a terrible mood, taking out his own frustration on his child by yelling or getting overly angry about something that was really not a big deal. The child experiences this behavior firsthand, and in turn seeks out someone they consider weaker to compensate for the feeling of powerlessness they now have. Maybe the next target is a sibling, maybe it's a classmate, but the bottom line is that we see a cycle of bullying that very often originates in the home by the parents. We can see that bullying begets bullying, and by recognizing this fact we can work to break the cycle.

Effects of Bullying

You've probably noticed that I've mentioned confidence and self-esteem quite a few times in this chapter. The reason is that these qualities are absolutely critical for anyone to have, but their importance is exponential in children. Bullying literally strips a child of their confidence and self-esteem little by little until there's nothing left.

In my own bullying experience I can remember how the incidents with my cousin and aunt stayed with me for many years. In grade school I was a target - I never stood up for myself and felt like I was always being picked on. I didn't have many friends, and felt like I was all alone. It was a terrible feeling, and sadly one that many children experience every day. I'm sure we can all agree that no child should be made to feel inferior, and that bullying shouldn't be ignored, so now we can take the next step of looking at ways to prevent bullying before it's too late.

Bully Prevention

The first suggestion I have for parents to combat bullying, and the ultimate prevention strategy in my opinion, is to take the time and connect with your kids. When I say connect I don't mean just have a talk or two and assume things are ok. It's not enough just to be living under the same roof - you have to be there *for* them, you have to be there *with* them, and they have to know it. I can be sitting in a room with a hundred people, it doesn't mean I'm connecting with them. Sleeping under the same roof doesn't prove you're involved in their life, it just means you live in the same house.

So connect with your kids and make the effort to understand what they're going through. Find out about the good things that are happening, the bad things, and how to help them cope with things they can't handle on their own. Make sure they know that you're willing to help them, that you'll take steps to resolve their issues as best you can. Remember, going home tired after working a long day doesn't make you an amazing parent. What makes you an amazing parent is going home tired after a long day and still taking the extra time to get to know your child.

The second suggestion I want to make as an effort to combat or prevent bullying is to enroll your child in a martial arts program. I say this with 100% understanding that my opinion may be completely bias, but I think that martial arts is hands down the best way to arm your child with the tools necessary to defend themselves against bullying when you're not able to be with them. When I say defend I don't mean just learning to punch and kick, (although those skills can be helpful depending on the type of bullying happening), but rather the mental aspects of martial arts.

We've established that bullying is just as much, if not more so, about the psychological effects as the physical effects. Martial arts training is unique in the sense that students learn psychological defense right along with physical defense, making it the perfect formula for bullyproofing. In martial arts the curriculum is specifically developed to focus on things like confidence, self-esteem, and pride in oneself. These lessons directly combat the tools bullies use, providing students with the means to cease being targets.

I've shared my personal experiences with bullying with you in this chapter, so I'll also share how I was able to break the cycle I was in. For me, as you might have guessed, it was martial arts training.

In the 6th grade I started martial arts training and my life changed. My confidence went up, my self-esteem went up, and my entire sense of self-worth went up. I was taught that I was special, and all of a sudden the bullying stopped. I never went up to my bullies and said, "Okay, now we can fight. I know karate!" I didn't have to - I just learned how to be me and believe in myself, and things fell into place.

To wrap things up, bullying is a real problem and should be addressed head on. It takes all forms, and one of the most common yet most overlooked form is bullying in the home. Just remember that as a parent you have the ability to combat bullying by being there for your kids and working together with them to make sure they get to live the happy and healthy lives they deserve. I wish you the best of luck, and also encourage you to seek out advice and guidance from other people who have valuable knowledge to share - you don't have to do it alone.

Juan Colon is the owner and Chief Instructor of Championship Martial Arts in Winter Springs, FL. His years of experience teaching kids has led to becoming a community leader and regular contributor to local schools. His martial arts and after school programs at Championship Martial Arts have won awards in the local area among parents.

For more information, visit www.cmatuskawilla.com.

CHAPTER 4: BULLYPROOFING STARTS WITH THE FAMILY

BY JO FULLER & OSHEN DUNCAN
HIGH WYCOMBE, BUCKINGHAMSHIRE
UNITED KINGDOM

Just as bullying awareness is on the rise in the United States it's also growing here in the United Kingdom. Similar to the United States we're seeing increased press coverage of bullying in the media, on the Internet, in the news, in the newspaper - just everywhere. When we opened our martial arts school eight years ago we decided to take a different approach to martial arts training and combating bullying than what others were doing. We knew we'd be touching the lives of hundreds of children, and felt that we needed to focus on the entire family as opposed to individual children in order to provide the most beneficial training experience. By using the idea of whole family training we've seen tremendous results in bullying awareness and prevention in our academy.

To understand a problem like bullying you've first got to define it. This is made a bit more complicated in the UK, in part because bullying is slightly different here than in the US. The dynamic is different because in the UK it's generally understood that kids go through something of a hazing ritual in schools, almost like a rite of passage. It's expected and usually condoned as a tradition, but in recent years we've seen an alarming increase in the severity of the hazing. In the past the hazing was normally isolated to verbal exchanges that were fairly innocent by today's standards. Recently the hazing has progressed to the point of ongoing and intentionally cruel provoking, even to the point of death threats and physical attacks in some cases. So the question here becomes when does hazing cross the line from acceptable to bullying? The question is even more important when we realize that the longer it takes to draw the hard line on bullying the more work will be needed to be done to fight it. Bullying is already on the rise, and as it grows it will continue to get worse and become and endless and continuing cycle for our kids.

There's also the issue of different types of bullying rising that were never an issue when we were growing up. Until the late 1980s we didn't really have racial bullying because we weren't very diverse. That's changed now, and when someone starts making fun of race as part of hazing that could be an example of crossing the line. Also, social media has helped change the face of bullying. When we were younger it was all done face-to-face whereas now there's a lot of bullying done through technology, which can oftentimes be nastier than what would be said in person.

Because of the multi-faceted nature of bullying we say that the way to define bullying is by looking at the suspect behavior and asking if it's consistent and persistent. In attempting to differentiate bullying from your normal hazing, what we've found is that hazing isn't done relentlessly or with harmful intent. Hazing isn't persistently going after someone, but more of a one-off insult or verbal jab here and there. With hazing there's also more of a back and forth as opposed to one person being the lone target of hurtful words or actions. So in the end, our best way of defining bullying is by saying it's made up of consistent and persistent words or actions that are done for the purpose of hurting another person.

The Struggles in Schools

Although the two of us have our own personal definition of bullying, as a country the UK is still struggling to agree upon a blanket statement of what bullying is. Likewise, schools are having a similar struggle in trying not only to differentiate between hazing and bullying, but also being able to explain the differences to kids in an easy to understand and straightforward way. This leads to confusion for the kids, but also miscommunication and tension between teachers and parents.

Teachers expect parents to step in and handle issues with their own children, but it seems that nowadays many parents feel they should be able to sit back and let teachers deal with bullying issues in schools. They expect the teacher to take care of things and resolve any issues. The teacher expects the parent to step in, the parent expects the teacher to deal with it, and the truth is the school system doesn't give the teachers the power they need to do anything really.

We think a major problem in this cycle is, and we hate to say it about our own country, but we think we've become very much a nanny state. When we were younger we had teachers who would nip bad behavior in the bud before it became an issue. If a teacher saw something happening they could clip a child in the ear and say that's not appropriate. Bad behavior was addressed early on and in no uncertain terms. We're not saying that's what needs to happen now, but we've gone from teachers having that kind of control to having to coddle and comfort instead of discipline when necessary. With all of this to consider, we've found that with schools having so little control it's really up to the families to fill the void and step up for their kids.

A Solution That Works

As we said, schools don't have the ability to protect our children against bullying right now. Instead, bullyproofing has to start in the home by focusing on spending time together as a family. When we say spending time together we mean really taking the time to engage and be a part of each other's lives. It's about quality, not quantity. It doesn't matter as much the specific amount of time as a family you spend together, it's whether that time spent is high quality. It's spending time listening to each other, being nonjudgmental, and being able to communicate openly without the fear of being told off. Some people might call it verbal vomit, just being able to unload anything and everything through dialogue.

The reason this type of family time is so important is that it really drives home that dynamic family relationship and commitment to

64

togetherness. It can be mom and dad, brothers and sisters, aunts and uncles, grandparents, or whoever else has a part in raising the kids. It's all about building those strong, trusting bonds so that kids are able to open up to parents and families about what's going on in their day-to-day lives. It gives kids the chance to express what they're feeling or thinking without being afraid of being told off for any reason.

Remember, your kids spend a great deal of time at school, which is also where most bullying incidents occur. By spending quality family time with one another you're giving your kids more opportunities to open up and let you be aware of what's going on with them in the places you can't be. By taking the time to get to know your kids in this way you'll also get a great chance to know them better. This will make you even more keen to notice when changes occur in your child's behavior that could signal deeper issues, like retreating from normal activities or self-harming.

Why Family Time Works

There are lots of reasons why quality family time is a solution that works to make your kids bullyproof. One is that by spending time together you get to know each other better. You learn about each other's quirks, faults, and positive qualities. This is huge, especially for siblings. Many families discount the idea that siblings can bully each other, but it definitely happens. Spending quality time together, especially in a group activity, helps kids to recognize and accept each other's faults no matter what.

This is also the reason we recommend group activities as the quality family time to participate in. You get these little extras that are so important, things that you wouldn't get in doing more individualized activities. While there are many different activities to choose from, we of course recommend martial arts. Any group activity is ok, but because of the success of martial arts we have to say it's the best choice.

Another reason family time via group activities works is because it's physical as well as mental. You're exercising the mind along with the body. An example of the mental benefit is the communication practice you can get. Not just verbal, but also non-verbal. You learn to read people, to read the clues in their expressions and posture that show you more about them and how they're feeling. These non-verbal cues lead to better overall communication as a family and a deeper connection with one another.

These days we don't get nearly enough practice in reading people to communicate. Everything is so digitally focused these days - Facebook, cell phones, text messages - we don't have the same amount of face-to-face interaction that we used to. It's important to focus on this communication because this is what will give you a better idea of when something is off with your child and you need to make sure you talk to them about it.

Finally, using group activities for quality family time works because you're able to surround yourself with like-minded people. For example, at Tiger Martial Arts you're not on your own - you're among other families who are also there to train and spend time together. This gives a sense of community and camaraderie, but also let's you see other family dynamics. As a parent you can look at another family and realize you're not alone in the struggles or joys you're feeling with your own family. Kids can look at other kids and see that they're also an older sibling, middle sibling, younger sibling, and identify with each other. It gives people common ground and an opportunity to learn about themselves through working with others in a safe, comfortable environment. In an activity like this where everyone in the family is involved, no one has a chance to feel left out or cast aside. Again, strong family bonds and connections are instrumental in making your child bullyproof.

Whether you're a parent in the US or the UK, bullying for kids today is a different thing than it was for us. It's more prevalent and yet in many ways harder to define. It comes in many forms, ranging from blatant and face-to-face to anonymous and online. It's nastier and more vicious now than ever before, and with these new changes come more dangers to watch for. Depression, self-harm, even suicides are all examples of things that can happen as a result of bullying.

Instead of waiting for bullying to show up and dealing with it after the fact be proactive and take steps to bullyproof your child before it's an issue. Don't rely on schools or others to take care of it for you, but step into the role of parent wholeheartedly and give your child what they need - someone to be there for them. Take the time to participate in activities as a family to keep those precious avenues of communication alive, and always maintain a supportive and loving presence in their lives. Seek out activities, like the martial arts, that put you in contact with other families that can also be a resource when you need them. Remember that the more time you spend with your kids the better job you'll be able to do at making them bullyproof.

Jo Fuller and Oshen Duncan are the owners and instructors at Tiger Martial Arts in High Wycombe, Buckinghamshire, United Kingdom. Their unique program focuses on working with families as a whole learning martial arts together. As parents themselves, Jo and Oshen are well aware of the devastating long-term effects that bullying can cause for children, as well as adults.

For more information, visit www.tigermartialarts.co.uk

CHAPTER 5: IS IT BULLYING? OR A BAD DAY?

BY RICHARD HILL
KILLEEN, TEXAS

I'm proud to be known as a business owner who is a trusted source for parents looking for information and training to bullyproof their kids. As a lifelong martial artist I've seen more than my fair share of bullying cases, and my expertise has allowed me to gain a great deal of knowledge and skill that I'm delighted to pass on through classes at my academy as well as numerous bully prevention seminars I've provided in the community. My experience has also shown me that there is a great deal of misconception out there about topics such as what bullying actually is, the right and wrong ways kids are taught to protect themselves against bullying, and even the positive and negative sides of how bullying is handled by parents, teachers, and the school systems.

One of the hard things about this subject of bullying is that the definition of what bullying is can vary greatly from person to person. For every person who says bullying is the worst thing in the world and a global epidemic there is another person who says it's not a big deal. Personally, I'm of the opinion that bullying is in fact a very big deal, and its importance is near and dear to my heart because of the children and families I've worked with over the years.

In my experience the definition of bullying is an occurrence that happens when someone is trying to make themselves look or feel superior by making someone else look or feel inferior. A bully is someone who wants control and they will take that control any way they can. They seek out targets they perceive as weaker than themselves because they lack something in their own life - self-esteem, control, security - or one of many other issues. The bottom line is that bullies are people who willfully push others down because of something they lack in their own lives.

Why Do Bullies Bully?

Unfortunately there may not be any blanket answer to this question, but the majority of bullying cases I've seen happen because the bully needs to feel control over someone else to compensate for a lack of control in their own life. Maybe the kid doing the bullying has an older sibling at home who is always picking on them, or it could even be a parent displaying bully-like behavior or abuse. So the kid we see as a bully is feeling weak and insecure at home, having their self-esteem broken down more and more each day. Then this kid gets out of that home environment and goes to school, away from their own bully, and they're able to find what they've been lacking - a victim who's weaker than themselves. The kid who is now a bully at school has learned the behavior from home and is perpetuating the cycle.

Is It Bullying, or Just a Bad Day?

One of the most common questions I get from people in regards to bullying is what the difference is between a bully and someone who's just having a bad day. Look, we all have bad days. We all have those times where we just want to lash out at someone - it could be a complete stranger or a dear loved one - just because we're in a bad mood. We might say or do mean things because we aren't feeling great. The differences between having a bad day and being a bully are the frequency and the feelings behind the actions.

Frequency means just that - how often you act in what may be seen as a bullying way. If you have a bad day once in a while that's normal. It's also normal to feel badly about it, which is where the feelings side comes in. People who have a bad day may say or do something mean enough to be close to a bullying event in that moment, but in the end they have a conscience and that's the difference. They apologize, say they can't believe they acted like that, and really mean it when they say it. They didn't actively go out looking for someone to unleash their frustration on. It's just that the events of the day were too much and they vented in the wrong way. For non-bullies these situations don't happen every day, and almost everyone has them.

Bullies, on the other hand, enjoy what they do because of how it makes them feel. They get off on hurting other people because it gives them a feeling they're lacking in their own life. They don't have remorse for their behavior, and they feed off of their victim's suffering. Because they get what they need from their actions bullies continue to go after their victims over and over again without letting up. So looking at those two key areas, the frequency of events and feelings behind them, it's actually pretty easy to see what constitutes bullying vs. just having a bad day.

Becoming Bullyproof

Since bullying has become something of a hot button issue in recent years it seems as if there are more theories, programs, trainings, and philosophies than ever about how to protect kids against it. Some of these are wonderful, and have been real world tested and proven effective in keeping kids safer. That being said, there are also a LOT of these so-called bully preventers out there that range from silly to downright dangerous for kids to use.

I came across one program in particular a few years ago that stands out to me as one that I'd consider dangerous. In this particular program a kid was taught to agree with a bully who insulted them. For example, the bully says, "Man, that's an ugly shirt. I can't stand that shirt." The program taught the kid being bullied to respond with something like, "Yeah, it's kind of ugly I guess, but your shirt's really great!" The kid being bullied would basically make a joke about himself or herself, which is just some of the absolute worst advice I've ever heard. A kid who's being bullied should never be taught to do that. They may already feel put down, and now they're being told to make fun of themselves even more than the bully did. It also makes them appear to be even more of a victim, and the more they look like a victim the more control a bully has. The bully doesn't see this scenario as a situation where they lose, but a situation where what they said made the victim agree with him. Now not only is the bully laughing, so is everyone else - so this technique actually gives the bully even more power.

Instead of looking like a victim, kids should be taught to stand up for themselves. Let's use the same example of a bully saying the victim's shirt is ugly. We should be teaching kids to have the confidence to say things like, "You don't like my shirt? So what. I like my shirt. My friends like my shirt. It's ok that you don't like my shirt, I don't really care." They need to be able to speak like this and be forceful about it, standing tall and looking the bully in the eyes. They shouldn't retreat or slink off without saying anything in their defense because the "just walk away" method doesn't work, either. Kids need to be able to speak their mind and stand up for themselves, then walk away when they choose to as opposed to slinking away feeling ashamed. They need to have this whole demeanor about them that says they're not a victim, not an easy target, and that's what they should be practicing.

I say practice because that's actually an important piece of bullyproofing, and one that often goes overlooked. We can't expect kids to just know this stuff - they need to work on it and develop their skills just like they would in reading or math. If they don't practice, they won't get good at it. There's an old saying we have in martial arts that "perfect practice makes perfect". Well, that's the case here. If you practice the wrong things you're not going to improve, but if kids practice how to become bullyproof the right way then they'll become much better at it. This is also an area parents should be focusing on, helping their kids practice this level of confidence. They could do it at home, or enroll them in an activity like martial arts, but it's definitely an important piece of the puzzle.

Parents, Teachers, and Schools

I mentioned that kids are all too often being taught how to handle bullying incorrectly, and the truth is that a lot of that comes from parents, teachers, and schools. For example, the school district where I live has a zero tolerance policy on bullying. In compliance with this policy the kids in school are told that when they're being bullied they should go tell an adult. On paper that seems like a great idea - in practice it's anything but. What happens is that many times the bullying incidents are reported and then written off as "kids being kids" by the school staff. Worse, in the cases that do get looked into, our school district's zero tolerance policy says that with a bullying situation both students get in trouble. So we tell kids to stand up for themselves and protect themselves, but now they have to worry about being in trouble for doing so. The good kid who doesn't want any issues has to make the choice of standing up for themselves and facing repercussions from the school or taking the bullying and facing the physical and emotional repercussions. This is just a wrong way to do things.

Whether this is how your school district works or not it can still serve as an example of mixed messages. As a parent it's crucial to have discussions with your child about what your school's policies are and how you want your child to handle bullying situations that come up. Don't be too quick to jump to the "kids being kids" reasoning. Take the time to hear your child out and see if the pattern they describe points to bullying. Talk to your child about what level of self-defense is appropriate verbally and physically, and how you'll help them and be there for them if anything happens. I'm not advocating fighting, but I am saying it's important to make sure you're protecting your child by allowing them to have the freedom to protect themselves with their words or their actions.

Bullying is a major problem and one we all have a shared responsibility to fight. I really believe that as a community we can eliminate bullying, but we have to come together to do so. Adults have to understand bullying so they can teach their children about it - what to do, what not to do, how to stand up against it - then, as those kids grow up, they'll be more aware. Kids are the future - we all know that. So if we're able to change the way kids are thinking about bullying then maybe, in the next generation, they'll be the community that finally defeats it. Ultimately it's your decision as a parent how to handle the subject of bullying, but I urge you to take a stand. We see statistics rising every day, every week, every month of kids being bullied and taking their lives because they feel worthless and that nothing is being done to help them. They don't see anybody standing up for them - let's make sure they see us.

Richard Hill owns Synergy Karate Academy in Killeen, Texas. Richard has been a student of the martial arts for 29 years. He started his martial arts journey in 1986 in Shorinji Kempo and Jiujitsu.

In 1989 he joined the US Army and spent 20 years as a Soldier retiring from active duty in 2009. He is a combat veteran and decorated soldier. He did four tours to combat zones prior to his retirement.

For more information, visit www.synergykarateacademy.com.

CHAPTER 6: THE IN-SCHOOL RESPONSE TO BULLYING

BY ERIN LAURAINE
COTTAGE GROVE, OREGON

A passion of mine has always been working with children. Being a martial arts instructor for over a decade has allowed me to pursue that passion and touch the lives of countless students in my care. In recent years I've noticed the subject of bullying coming up more and more often, and my position as a martial arts school owner has given me tremendous insight into the world of bullying. I consider working with children to be one of my specialties, but when it comes to the subject of bullying I'm also very well versed in understanding how school policies work.

Personally speaking, the bulk of my experience with bullying has really happened through working with students. I grew up in a home-educated environment so my perspective on bullying and the way it's handled in schools is unique in the sense that it's very much objective, looking at it from the outside in so to speak. This perspective has allowed me to better understand the mechanics of how schools handle bullying problems in general, as well as how they regulate and try to control specific issues.

As a result of my work with children I've come to understand what students experience through the various stages of development, beginning as early as elementary school and continuing throughout their lives. In over a decade of working with these students, I've seen how bullying can have a long-term impact on someone, sometimes even lasting through adulthood. The prevalence of bullying in schools has led me to focus much of my time learning about how exactly schools handle bullying - or in some cases, how they don't - and also what parents can be doing to protect their children from bullying.

Understanding Bullying in the Schools

First of all, I think we can agree on a general definition of bullying as being intentional ongoing or repeated actions by one person done for the purpose of making another person feel badly about themselves. Let's also assume that we agree that bullying can be physical or emotional, and that there is no real cookie cutter approach to facilitate every instance of bullying that occurs. That being said, certain constants can be seen in how schools handle bullying and the systems in place to do so.

First, at the broadest end of the spectrum, we have the United States Department of Education (US DOE). Their main occupation, in terms of bullying, is on civil rights laws. Without getting into details, these laws essentially say that all students have a right to a safe place to learn that is free from harassment or discrimination.

These are often the basic rights that bullies violate as they seek out targets to go after.

Next, there are individual states. At this level, individual states decide what standards from the US DOE they want to expand or adapt for their individual needs. I believe that for the most part most states have adapted their own verbiage for their anti-bullying policies and try to be very specific about what classifies as bullying and harassment.

Finally, at the most focused point, there are individual school districts. The school districts are required to, at the minimum, follow the state laws that are derived from the federal laws. Often, individual school districts expand even more on state laws and are able to carefully craft programs that meet their specific requirements.

It's crucial that parents understand how bullying policies travel down the education chain of command and what their own school district's individual policies are. A district may be very specific about what constitutes bullying, and parents must be able to communicate with their children about these rules. Also, districts may go into great detail about what their reporting procedures are, what the follow-up process entails, potential for appeal proceedings, a chain of command for who needs to be contacted, what information needs to be recorded digitally or submitted in writing, etc. These elements can become very, very specific to each state, and can become more detailed as you get into varying school districts and even individual schools. So parents really need to know where their child is, what the district anti-bullying requirements are, and what the school's own requirements are.

What Can Schools Do?

One of the most common questions I hear from parents is, "With such a big issue like bullying, how much can a school really do to combat it?" There are a number of programs out there, and many are quite effective. One program that I've seen some great results with is the OLWEUS bullying prevention program. OLWEUS gives ongoing tools and training to the entire school's staff - teachers, janitors, administrators, etc. - and from there also passes the training to students and parents. Again, it's a great program if it's given the time and effort required to let it be successful.

The truth is that there are many similar programs schools can adopt to combat bullying, but one of the main obstacles they face in implementing any program is limitation of resources. Granted, not all schools face these resource issues, but many do. Schools are limited on staff, time, funds, and resources to run a lasting and successful anti-bullying program. Sadly, some studies have actually shown that in schools that have implemented anti-bullying programs only half of the staff members were adequately trained. As a result, the programs weren't effective due to being understaffed.

So the issue isn't so much that anti-bullying programs don't work, it's more that they can't be implemented effectively. The lack of resources is a major hurdle, and an important one to get over so that programs that do work can have a chance to prove their value. This shortfall, to me, demonstrates the need for more community involvement. With limited resources a school's administration can only do so much, so this is a great opportunity for parents and families to step up and donate their time in order to fill in the support gaps.

Many school districts are rightfully looking to the community to be more involved in their anti-bullying campaigns and strategies. Community-type outreach programs are gaining traction as more districts are realizing that bullying is one of those topics that an entire community can rally around, as opposed to the school district going it alone. I've seen examples where parents even volunteer to sort of patrol the school and be more present, providing more eyes in areas teachers can't always see everything like recess, cafeterias, hallways, and stairwells. I believe that while the onus of taking care of bully issues falls on school administration, parental involvement is also very important.

What Can Parents Do?

Honestly, for a parent to be involved in bully-proofing their children they really just need to try to be more involved in their lives, especially at school. By becoming more involved in their children's school lives a parent is able to build a different kind of rapport with schoolteachers and administrators. Instead of coming in only when there are problems, parents that are involved in the school come across as looking for ways they can contribute to solutions as opposed to expecting the school to do all of the work. Joining a PTA or PTO group is a great way of showing support, and these groups really reinforce the anti-bullying messages in any school. They're really set up perfectly to reach out to the community and help keep kids safer.

That being said, I understand that many parents really don't have the time for a lot of volunteering. Of course that's a situation lots of people face. However, you should know that you don't necessarily have to volunteer your time to be a resource for your child and their school. Just taking the time to really understand the school's policies, talking them over with your child, and being available to talk to the teachers if issues do arise will go a long way in working together to combat bullying in the schools.

Summary

Each state, school district, and individual school can vary greatly on how they handle bullying issues. As a parent it's crucial to understand your school's policies, talk about those policies with your kids, and do what you can to support the school's efforts to combat bullying. Schools can't win the fight against bullying on their own, but with your support you can help create a system that will keep your children safer. Along with that, always try to maintain open and honest dialog with your kids about bullying, and make sure the lines of communication are clear between you, your kids, and their teachers. We can absolutely combat bullying, but none of us can do it alone.

Erin Lauraine owns Lauraine's ATA Martial Arts in Cottage Grove, Oregon. Erin is a 5th Degree Black Belt in Taekwondo with over 17 years of experience.

Her passions have included adaptive training for students with limited cognitive or physical abilities, as well as community engagement.

For more information, visit www.atacottagegrove.com

CHAPTER 7: WHY MOST "ANTI-BULLY" PROGRAMS DON'T WORK

BY JOHN NOTTINGHAM
PHOENIX, ARIZONA

Bullying is an important issue to me. So important, actually, that my entire career could be said to have begun as a result of bullying. I own and operate USA Martial Arts in Phoenix, Arizona, and I love what I do. One of the primary reasons I started in martial arts was that I was bullied as a kid, and I understand that feeling of powerlessness. Participating in martial arts changed my life so much that I now devote myself to sharing anti-bullying strategies with others. My training and experience have culminated in a program I call "Bullyproof Vest", which is based on effective, common-sense practices (even though they are probably contrary to many of the mainstream views currently being advocated).

Is Bullying Really a Big Deal?

The short answer is, yes, of course it is! However, I do realize that some people think bullying really isn't that big of a problem. They say kids just need to suck it up or that people just need to be tougher. But this mentality does not address the struggle that many children face every day as they are taunted, intimidated, and even threatened by those society would call "bullies". It certainly doesn't equip them to respond to the problem effectively. I believe bullying is not only harmful to the person being bullied, it's damaging to the perpetrator as well. Bullying is also detrimental to society as a whole and has been around since the beginning of human existence. We need to do what we can to combat it, and I believe the best approach is to empower individuals as opposed to implementing the current school-wide anti-bullying programs.

Anti-Bullying Programs Don't Work

The sweeping, school-wide anti-bullying programs don't work, and this has been proven through several major scientific studies. Part of the problem lies in the way people have been taught to think about bullying and the programs that go along with it. First, bullying isn't a clinical diagnosis (although many are now attempting to make it so) but rather a social label. This is ironic because many in the anti-bullying movement say it's wrong to name-call, and yet here we are redirecting the name-calling back at the bully -- it just doesn't make sense!

Anti-bullying isn't the first example, but rather another in a long line of ill-conceived programs that have had the opposite result of what was intended. For example, the DARE program (Drug Awareness Resistance Education), was a target-specific program designed to keep kids off drugs. Billions of tax dollars were thrown down this well-intentioned hole, and we now have long-term studies that show that some schools with strong DARE programs actually had increases in drug sales and use.

Another example is a program that put fear in the hearts of an entire generation of kids: Stranger Danger. This program taught kids that all strangers were bad and should be avoided. There's the story of the lost little boy in Utah who was passed several times by rescuers because he was hiding from the strangers he saw. He thought he was in danger from the very people who were there to rescue him! We terrified a generation of children and their parents by promoting fear of things that were unlikely to happen instead of educating them about real risk factors. We know that non-familial abductions are extremely rare, yet it has become a pervasive thought for parents. Even today the lingering effects of Stranger Danger keep parents from letting their kids go to the park or participate in certain activities. In reality these activities would make them safer, because when we learn to participate in calculated risk we learn how to better mitigate risk and unintended consequences. Social scientists and psychologists tell me that children who are taught how to participate in risk are safer, happier and more successful because they better understand how to calculate it. Unfortunately, this approach is the opposite of that taken by many national programs.

What is Happening in Bullying Efforts Today

These programs, along with anti-bullying programs, haven't worked mainly because they focus on the wrong things: victim culture, division, reporting on others, blaming, abdicating safety, and acting powerless. My issue with victim culture is that it robs children of their power and dignity and leaves them at risk for more abuse in the future. The combination of denial, blame and powerlessness is never a good defensive strategy - nor is it a happy way to live life.

Instead of creating solutions, what we create are even more complex problems than what we had to begin with. Today bullying is obviously a hot button issue, but it's often politically motivated. It isn't truly focused on getting measurable results, but is more of a feel-good movement. To get real results we have to be honest about bullying, but the programs being developed are not responding correctly to the reports we are receiving on the matter.

A great way to prove the political motivation of the current anti-bullying movement is to comment against it. You know what happens when you do? You get bullied! You're not allowed to disagree with the Establishment, because they're focused on this mission of eliminating bullying that's driven more by profits and politics than it is by science and facts. What we need to do is bring some realistic and practical thinking into the conversation so we can address the real problem instead of just trying to make ourselves feel better about it.

I don't doubt everyone's motives. Most people truly care and want to make a difference. I believe their hearts are in the right place, and I have the utmost respect for those who have been doing the hard work all these years to build resilience and self-esteem in children. But when it comes to programs to improve the wellbeing of our children, we need to be sure that our efforts are moving us in the right direction. I observed the multi-billion-dollar waste of money that was the DARE program, and I saw a generation of scared mothers and children because of the alarmism of Stranger Danger. The current anti-bullying movement smells the same to me. Again, billions of dollars are being spent on programs that aren't focusing on the right areas and are instead creating more complex problems.

Change the Focus

I've mentioned that we need to change the focus and ask the right questions; we need to change the way we think about bullying. I love to tell a story about Mother Teresa, someone you can't help but hold up as an extraordinary example of love and compassion. In this story, Mother Teresa was in a meeting, and there were anti-war protests happening in the streets near her. One of the protestors came running up to her and said, "Mother Teresa, how could you be here in this meeting? We need you with us at the anti-war rally!" Mother Teresa calmly said to the man, "Call me when it's a peace rally."

I think that's a pretty profound way to express the power that comes with a change in thinking. That's what the anti-bullying movement needs. Right now the thinking is mostly focused on victims. The anti-bullying movement highlights victims, and so that's what we see covered by the media. We also see this approach turning those victims into anti-heroes and attention-getters. Let's remember for a moment that almost every school mass-murderer has seen himself as a victim. People have the ability to commit horrible atrocities when they justify themselves as victims. We're focused on the wrong things and using the wrong methods to protect our kids. The result has been nothing short of catastrophic.

The Wrong Way to Bullyproof a Child

There are many wrong methods that different bullyproofing programs use, and I'll highlight a couple of them here. One strategy on the anti-bullying front essentially turns peers into informants, creating further division among students in schools. This method says, 'we have to have our bystanders tell on the bully'. In other words, 'we need to have kids reporting on everyone else'. This requires teachers to operate as police. So great! The outcome is totalitarianism and that's what we're teaching our children. Instead of giving them strategies that might be more difficult – but work! – we're content to take the easy way out and abdicate responsibility to other kids and teachers. Blame is at the foundation of the anti-bully movement and alarmism is one of its most pervasive tools. It makes it convenient to then blame teachers and school administrators when things go wrong. The result? More division, more blame, more conflict, and attorneys profiteering with lawsuits.

Other 'big ideas' include hanging up lots of anti-bullying posters, or holding big assemblies with clowns and magicians and whatever celebrity is focusing on bullying issues that week. All of these various programs drain taxpayer money and only make us feel good about taking action when in reality we're not doing anything substantial or lasting. We even have a conflict of interest when we maintain zero-tolerance policies while simultaneously trying to teach kids about tolerance. How can you teach tolerance with zero-tolerance policies at the forefront of current strategy?

The Right Way to Bullyproof a Child

In order to bullyproof kids properly, we need to change the foundation of the entire anti-bullying movement. Our focus must be on peace training, kindness training and character education.

The first step in changing the foundation of the whole approach is to start teaching kids how to put things in context. Children lack the ability to do that and therefore we need to help them. We need to teach them how to understand their feelings, and that compassion and empathy are important. This isn't a quick fix – and it's not going to come from a poster – but it's important for kids to know that words and ideas aren't always permanent judgment. We don't want to permanently label a person a bully, or believe that we're permanently labeled ourselves, but rather we should foster things like forgiveness, understanding and compassion. Of course there is the reality of having to deal with aggression or physical bullying when it happens, and there are tools for that too, but it begins with teaching kids how to love, be tolerant and establish mutual respect.

Bullyproof Strategies

One of the ways we can impart these ideas at the most fundamental level is to teach boundary-setting, which is a critical life skill. If we don't teach kids about boundaries when they're young, we set them up for a lifetime of failure. We overprotect them, we coddle them, and we feel good about the protection we give, but we don't teach them how to protect themselves by creating boundaries and understanding how they work. I know adults who are highly educated, but who are also completely derelict in this area. They have no ability to protect themselves from bullying behaviors – and it goes all the way up to the corporate level.

It all begins by setting boundaries, owning our own mental and physical space, and learning that others have the right to their opinions and space as well. We don't always have to agree with everyone, but can't we have non-adversarial discussions? We can disagree without being disagreeable and teach our kids about boundary setting in the process. This is a radical shift from the rhetoric of the current anti-bullying movement.

Part of mental boundary-setting is teaching kids that their value doesn't come from other people. Right now we have a generation of kids that has been told that words can destroy them. I would never want my children to believe that words can destroy who they are, because that puts all of the power into other people's opinions about them. Instead, we can allow other people to have their opinions and we have the option to reject them. It's OK for somebody else to have a different opinion and we can know that it doesn't have to affect us. Maybe they're having a horrible day or maybe they have a horrible life, but our value doesn't lie in someone else's opinion of us. The pervasive message of the anti-bullying movement is the opposite: that we have to somehow control how others perceive us (as if we could even do that). We shouldn't even try to control the perceptions of others lest we risk becoming bullies ourselves! It's a dangerous road to go down, and therefore it is not a methodology I advocate.

Different Courses of Action

The approach we take in our anti-bullying program at USA Martial Arts is to teach kids that their personal value and the way they perceive themselves should never be wrapped up in someone else's opinion of them, and I've got a great way to demonstrate how different this approach is from a typical anti-bullying program. There's a popular demonstration that people do in assemblies or classrooms where the presenter has students write down horrible insults on a piece of paper. The presenter assists by giving them ideas for nasty, horrible things they could say to others and then has the kids crumple up the paper. Next, the kids are told to uncrumple the paper and flatten it back out, the point being that the wrinkles or scars from the words are still there and that they can never be taken back.

What a harmful message to send to children – that they are permanently damaged or scarred from someone saying something negative about them. This approach is exactly what the current anti-bullying movement is all about, though. Current "experts" are capitalizing on a victim culture, creating kids who see themselves as injured and permanently wounded from these offensive words.

What we do instead is a similar exercise, but I use a $20 bill instead of plain paper. I insult it, yell at it, crunch it, wad it up, rub it in my armpit, step on it, and all kinds of ridiculous things. Then I hold it up and ask who still wants it. Some kids initially say, "eww, gross!" But as soon as I tell them they can take this $20 right now and go spend it, the hands shoot up to take it. I say, 'But I was horrible to this $20 bill! I said terrible things to it, I stepped all over it...why do you still want it?' The kids want it because it still works - it still has value even though it went through some tough stuff. I explain to them that their value works the same way: their inherent value never changes because they get roughed up or bad things happen to them. Carl Jung said, "I am not what happened to me. I am what I choose to become". This offers hope and healing. To me, that's a much better message to be teaching our kids.

Giving Them the Tools

The tools we give to our children need to actually work, not just make us feel good as parents and educators. The goal of our anti-bullying program is to teach children how to stay soft on the inside – kind, compassionate, understanding, and forgiving – but also to carry the tools they need to protect themselves. This empowers them to put on their "Bullyproof Vest", so when insults come their way they bounce right off. The main focus is to build their confidence, self-esteem, and sense of self-worth above all. By doing this we're able to create a mindset in our kids that they can't control other people's thoughts, but they absolutely can control their own.

Our students learn these skills through instruction, role-playing and practice. It's no different than teaching kids about fire safety and practicing what to do in an emergency. By focusing on skills that work and empower our kids, they gain abilities that can protect them from bullying. We may not be able to stop kids from getting picked on, but we can train them and give them the tools to respond appropriately. We can teach kids to retain their personal value and walk away from the situation without feeling like they surrendered their dignity. The anti-bullying movement promotes blame and powerlessness. It's the message that you cannot protect yourself and that others must always come to your rescue. It is devoid of problem-solving skills, responsibility, dignity and most importantly common-sense safety. Right now we're telling kids that they don't have any inherent value apart from the opinions of other people. We teach them to walk away without feeling right about it, or to rat out other kids immediately. What ends up happening is that the kids being bullied still feel terrible and now they are also being ostracized. Worse yet, they become "heroes" of a sort that focuses on glorifying the art of victimization – and the gruesome cycle continues. It can equate to a social death, and time and again, I have seen the way it damages self-esteem.

We have to give kids the tools to become bullyproof, and part of that is changing the victim mentality. We have a victim-centric culture now that is perpetuated by the current anti-bullying movement. Let's change the focus from victim to hero. We put kids in a program and build their confidence. They start standing taller; they engage people and make eye contact; and they are able to communicate non-verbally that they are not an easy target. They no longer fit the victim profile - they become a hero. Best of all, these skills and dignity and resilience can stay with them for life. This hero culture is what we want to continue developing, because a hero does what's right. A hero takes what he has learned and continues to spread those skills, even to the point of standing up for people who can't stand up for themselves. She has the guts to go sit down with the kid who is all alone at lunch, or to stand up for the kid who's not being invited to play at recess. That's hero culture! You don't get that by making heroes out of victims but rather by making heroes out of heroes – out of people exhibiting the behavior you want to see more of. That's what we should be encouraging through the tools and strategies we give our kids.

A Word on Bullies

By now you've got a pretty good idea that my views and methods are a bit contrarian to others with which you might be familiar. I'd also like to offer a different way to think about bullies themselves. Right now the main method of bully prevention is essentially bully-hunting. I've been teaching child safety for a long time, and my biggest concern with bully-hunting is what would be found if we were to dig deeper into bullying behaviors. A major indicator of an abused child is, in fact, the displaying of bullying behaviors. Many times these kids are getting bullied at home and then they go to school and bully others. It's a mistake to throw the baby out with the bathwater; it's a tragedy to write off these kids as "bullies" without trying to help them. The children who are labeled as bullies may be the ones who need us most because they have no one else advocating for them. If we start throwing people away, how can we hope to help them?

Bullying is an issue that we all must be aware of in order to combat it. I want to encourage everyone to take a step back and think about bullying in a different way. While the methods out there now are well-meaning, I think we're being taught to focus on the wrong things and ask the wrong questions. We owe it to our kids to take responsibility and prepare them for the world as effectively as possible. We need to create a hero culture instead of a victim culture.

To wrap it all up, love your children enough to teach them how to be resourceful problem solvers. Help them develop their social and emotional intelligence by empowering them with the ability to set personal boundaries. Teach them that their self-worth does not come from the opinions of others. They are valuable all on their own and they are worth protecting.

John Nottingham is the founder, President and Technical Director of USA Martial Arts in Phoenix, AZ. He was honored with the distinguished title "Master" in 1997. Master Nottingham, a 7th Degree Black Belt, was inducted into the International Hall of Fame on July 23, 2005. He holds multiple advanced degrees of Black Belt and numerous teaching credentials and certifications.

John developed the BullyProof Vest Program as a response to "anti-bully" programs that were proven ineffective. The BullyProof Vest program was developed as a peace process rather than the typical punitive process. Built on a foundation of bodyguard concepts, John Nottingham's BullyProof Vest program integrates elements of advanced threat assessment, effective boundaries, self defense, verbal judo, social and emotional intelligence.

For more information visit www.usa-martialarts.com

118

CHAPTER 8: CYBER-BULLYING — THE NEXT GENERATION OF BULLYING

BY BRETT LECHTENBERG
SANDY, UTAH

Over the years I've established myself as one of Utah's number one authorities in personal safety. My deepest passion lies in working with families to train them in strategies to stay safe in all aspects of their lives. I've taught a number of personal protection programs for children and adults, and one of the most common concerns families have is the issue of bullying. Bullying is one of the biggest topics we hear about these days. It's permeated our culture, existing not only in face-to-face incidents but also digitally. With the prevalence of things like social media and text messaging, cyber bullying is running rampant more than ever and families need to be aware of the issue as well as strategies to combat it.

What is Cyber Bullying?

People may have varying ideas of what bullying is. Personally, I define bullying as any repeated act from one person towards a target that causes that target to feel harassed, shamed, fearful of physical danger, or anything along those lines. Essentially bullying is generally an unwanted action by a person or persons, usually repeated more than once, that keeps a target in some sort of negative position.

Many people will immediately read those definitions and picture a schoolyard bully picking on other children. That's certainly a common form of bullying, but by no means the only one. In these technology driven days another form of bullying, known as cyber bullying, is increasing at an alarming rate. Generally, cyber bullying is very similar to physical bullying in its core definition. It's harassment or intentional embarrassment through some form of electronic medium like Facebook, Twitter, YouTube videos, Flickr images, etc. The difference is that there is no physical confrontation. The bullying is electronic, but it's still a repeated act of negative action towards a target.

Although not everyone is even aware of it, the reality is that cyber bullying is becoming the most dangerous and common type of bullying. One reason is that cyber bullying never goes away. A child may be in school for six hours a day, but cyber bullying doesn't have to happen at school. Actually, in my own opinion and from my research, cyber bullying doesn't really happen much at school. At school they tell the kids to turn their cell phones off. They also have limited access to computers, and the access they do have is typically monitored and in a structured environment. After school, though, is where we see the most problems. This is when kids have free access to their phones, tablets, computers, etc. If they decide they want to make a target out of someone, they can just sit and do it all day and all night if they like. It's a much bigger, scary, and more dangerous animal than "traditional" bullying.

Effects of Cyber Bullying

The effects of bullying on anyone, child or adult, can be devastating. However, most adults reach a stage in their lives where the opinions of others are a lot less important to them. They figure, "I've got a few good friends, that's great. I don't care about everybody else". Most kids don't have that same sense of self-esteem. They want to be liked, they want to be accepted. They want to be part of the cool social circle and "in" crowd, so when bullying happens it's very damaging to them. Kids, much more so than adults, are really affected by people making derogatory comments about them online.

For example, you've got Joey who is constantly being bombarded on Facebook, Twitter, and the rest about his appearance. Maybe he wears glasses, maybe he can't afford the newest style of clothes, whatever. With cyber bullying even more so than with traditional bullying, what we see happening next is people just piling onto Joey. One person makes a comment, then another, and soon we see a snowball effect where Joey now has what seems like his entire school commenting about his family being too poor to afford clothes for him.

From a child's perspective, this feels like the entire world is against them. Joey may have some support, but the positive voices are almost always quieter than the negative ones. Psychologically this is devastating for a child. A victim of bullying can experience negative effects like depression, physical illness, changes in personality, and even death. We've all heard stories about victims of bullying who were so traumatized by the constant barrage of negativity that they took their own life.

Signs of Cyber Bullying

Now that we've explored what bullying is and how it can affect kids, let's talk a little bit about signs parents should look for in order to catch bullying before it's too late. Watching for the signs of bullying can, admittedly, be difficult. Some of the main behaviors that surface while someone is being bullied include becoming withdrawn, wanting to stop going to school altogether, not hanging out with their normal group of friends, or pulling back from typical activities and actions.

The tricky thing is that all of these behaviors could be a sign of a teenager going through any one of many life stages. It becomes nearly impossible for a parent to just look at their child and think, "Hmmm, I think they're being bullied". A parent isn't a mind reader; they can't know what is actually happening in their child's life without being a part of their life. So while being mindful of the general signs of bullying is important, the only way to truly know if your child is being bullied is by talking to them.

Steps to Protect Against Cyber Bullying

This leads me into what is by far the most effective tool in protection against bullying, and that is consistent, continual, and open communication lines with your children, with their siblings, even with their friends. The idea is to be as tuned into your children's lives as possible, because it's the only way you're going to know for sure if they're having bullying issues. You have to be proactive.

Being proactive doesn't mean that I'm advocating for total control over your children's lives. Of course they need to have freedom, but as a parent it's your job to be an active participant in their life. For example, if your son or daughter wants to be on Facebook then make it a requirement that you're an unrestricted friend of theirs so you can see what is being posted on their account. Set rules about how they get to use social media, don't just sit back and assume they're responsible and mature enough to navigate issues that could arise.

Also, if your children are going to have a cell phone, tablet, or other device be upfront with them and let them know what your expectations are. When my wife and I gave our son his first cell phone we said, "Look, we're paying for this. You get to use it, but we get to monitor it whenever we want". We told him that that if he has an issue he can come to us, whether it's downloading some stupid app by accident or someone sends him an inappropriate or bullying text. We made sure he knew that if he came to us, with anything, he wouldn't be in trouble. If we found something and he didn't come to us, that's when there would be a problem.

It all goes back to open and honest communication. You don't have to be on your kids' devices every day, but monitor them once in a while and talk to them often about it. Be firm but fair and you'll be able to avoid confrontation while doing your job as a parent and protecting your family. Interact with your children, show them you're involved, follow them on Twitter, learn about Snapchat...the bottom line is that the best way to protect your children against bullying is to keep those lines of communication open.

What to Do If You Find Your Child is Being Cyber Bullied

If you find yourself in the unfortunate but common situation of having a child who is being bullied it's important to know what steps should be taken. First, reassure your child that you're going to take action, and really mean it. I've seen it happen many times where a parent tells their child they're going to take action and then they fall short. These are usually the parents who immediately give a laundry list of action steps, "I'm going to talk to your teacher, I'm going to talk to your principal, I need to contact the other kid's parents, I'm going to do X, I'm going to do Y, I'm going to do Z...". The reality is that so early on you have no idea how things will play out. Letting yourself become stressed, angry, and irrational doesn't help to deal with the situation, and in fact can make it worse. Instead, stay calm and tell your child, "Hey, I'm going to help you. I'm going to take action". Then you can make a real plan and go at it without being overly emotional and potentially adding to the problem.

The next thing to do is capture the information as quickly as possible. I call this step the Cyber Bully Information Capture System. This is a methodical system you go through where you capture and save anything that's come into your child's cell phone, computer, etc. Capture and save that information - whatever accounts, wherever possible. This is crucial because some information posted publicly may be able to be deleted by the bully, leaving you without proof. Once you have the information captured and saved, add time and date stamps wherever possible and make a presentation of everything you have. This information will be very important if you have to provide documentation for a principal, lawyer, police investigation, etc. You want to create a timeline, with an origination point if possible, in order to have as much information as possible if things escalate. It's much better to have and not need than to need and not have.

Finally, get rid of everything you can from your child's devices. You have the information saved, the next step is to try and distance your child from the effects of the bullying as soon as possible. Capture, save, and erase the information. If it's bad or threatening messages or texts, block the number of the person(s) sending the messages. If it's emails, block those emails; same with Facebook accounts and other social media. Whatever form the bullying has been coming from, however the bully is sending their information, block it to keep it away.

Also, understand that there are no guarantees that your child will be spared after the blocks take effect. People can find ways around your defenses if they're determined - setting up new profiles, recruiting others to join the bullying, etc. They might attack again, and you'll have to be diligent and block again. You should also try to stay up to date on the security features your child's devices have built into them. Look at the "readme" files on the Mac and PC platforms; they'll give you information about blocking things and restricting websites. Or just Google "top ten best security software programs for..." and fill in the blank with whatever you're trying to defend against. Ultimately, you may also have to think about making the decision of changing your child's information like their email account and phone number. If that happens, I'll go back again to reminding you to be open and honest with your child - keep those lines of communication open throughout the process.

Summary

The world is constantly changing, and cyber bullying is something that we as parents never really had to deal with growing up. It's important that we remain aware of the problem now, and that we let our children know they can come to us with any issues. The absolute most important thing is sitting down with your kids, talking with them, and making sure that they know you love and support them unconditionally. That is always going to be number one. I know that I might sound like a broken record at this point, but truly that will get you more results than anything else - making sure your kids know they can trust you and that you will take action if something happens. From there, really be willing and prepared to take whatever action is needed by having a plan for what to do before, during, and after your child comes to you with bullying concerns. We may not be able to stop bullying altogether, but we can and should be doing everything in our power to protect our children so they can stay happy and healthy.

Brett Lechtenberg is Utah's Leading Expert on Personal Safety. His martial arts school, Personal Mastery Martial Arts, is focused on developing individuals through leadership, communications skills, confidence building, family protection, and much more.

Brett is the best-selling author of The Anti Bully Program, The Anti-Cyber Bully Program, and Protecting Your Castle.

Brett continues his Personal Mastery Mission through his work with business owners and entrepreneurs to master their businesses and lives.

For more information visit www.brettlechtenberg.com

YOUR NEXT STEP:
THE BUTTERFLY EFFECT

Thank you for reading this book, the first in a series that is designed to raise awareness of the problem of the effects of bullying in our society.

While the contributing authors each have a very unique, and quite possibly, conflicting, opinion on the mechanics of becoming bullyproof, one thing is universal among all of the experts and leaders: it is up to us, as individuals in our communities to do something about it.

In your town, city or community there are numerous efforts to affect change to better the lives of kids in schools who are affected by bullying. There are organizations that will, for little or no cost, educate and advocate for kids to empower them to become their own heroes.

At this point you have a choice. You can put this book down, having collected the opinions of the best minds in bullying prevention, and you can say "Wow, that was terrific!" and go about your life as usual. And the natural consequence of this action will be that everything that has continued to be, will be.

Or, the other option is to do something. Do something in your community to make a difference. Whether it is to go to your local martial arts school and sign up your kid, or to attend a seminar with Tony Robbins to empower yourself, or even to create a support group that pledges to actively work to empower the people in your town. And the natural consequence of *this* action will be that something will be different.

136

You have probably heard of "The Butterfly Effect." It is the theory that small changes in a system can alter outcomes significantly. For example, the flapping of the wings of a butterfly on one side of the ocean (a seemingly insignificant action) can result in a drastic change in the trajectory of a hurricane.

What is your "butterfly effect" going to be?

How many heroes will be unleashed because of you?

It's up to you.

GETTING INVOLVED WITH THE BULLYPROOF PROJECT

The *Bullyproof: Unleash the Hero Inside Your Kid* book series is designed to raise awareness. However, awareness isn't enough. To effect true, lasting change in our communities, it requires action.

The contributing authors of the *Bullyproof* series are committed to bettering their hometowns through community involvement. Many are on speaking tours, school visits, or hold bullyproof classes. They are known as the Bully Experts in their town, the go-to source of real transformation in people.

The truth is that one can't read a book, or take one workshop, or attend one pep rally and become bullyproof. It takes time, effort, energy and commitment.

These contributing authors have missions in their businesses to help kids and adults become empowered, and the best way for them is to establish an ongoing working relationship with their clients and communities.

If you, like them, are completely committed to transforming your community and making it bullyproof, and you would like to be involved in a future volume of the *Bullyproof: Unleash the Hero Inside Your Kid* series, then we should talk.

Contact Alex at www.alexchangho.com or via email at alex@alexchangho.com and let's make a difference in our communities together.